Yoshi's Feast

by Kimiko Kajikawa

illustrated by Yumi Heo

Dorling Kindersley Publishing, Inc.

DK Ink

A Melanie Kroupa Book
Dorling Kindersley Publishing, Inc.
95 Madison Avenue, New York, New York 10016

Visit us on the World Wide Web at http://www.dk.com

Dorling Kindersley books are available at special discounts for bulk purchases for sales promotions or premiums. Special editions, including personalized covers, excerpts of existing guides, and corporate imprints can be created in large quantities for specific needs. For more information, contact Special Markets Dept., Dorling Kindersley Publishing, Inc., 95 Madison Ave., New York, NY 10016; fax: (800) 600-9098.

Library of Congress Cataloging-in-Publication Data

Kajikawa, Kimiko.
    Yoshi's feast / by Kimiko Kajikawa ; illustrated by Yumi Heo. —1st ed.
       p.   cm.
    "A Melanie Kroupa book."
    Summary: When Yoshi's neighbor, Sabu, the eel broiler, attempts to charge him for the delicious-smelling aromas he has been enjoying, Yoshi hatches a plan to enrich them both.
    ISBN 0-7894-2607-2
    [1. Neighborliness—Fiction. 2. Eels—Fiction. 3. Japan—Fiction.] I. Heo, Yumi, ill. II. Title.
PZ7.K117465Yo 2000
[E]—dc21
                                99-14754
                                CIP

Book design by Chris Hammill Paul. The illustrations are oil, pencil, and collage.
The text of this book is set in 18 point Calligraphic 421.

Printed and bound in U.S.A.

First Edition, 2000

10 9 8 7 6 5 4 3 2 1

In loving memory of my grandfather,
Motosuke Kajikawa —K.K.

In loving memory of my grandfather,
Harry Birnbaum —Y.H.

Yoshi's Feast was adapted from a story, "Smells and Jingles," in William Elliot Griffis's *Japanese Fairy World: Stories from the Wonder-lore of Japan* (J. H. Barhyte, 1880). The author thanks Japanese historian Kimiko Manes for her knowledge and assistance.

Long ago in the city of Yedo, there lived a fan maker named Yoshi who loved broiled eels.

Yoshi lived next door to Sabu, who broiled the most delicious-smelling eels in Yedo. But Sabu had few customers. His hibachi was difficult to find, for it was hidden away on a small street on the outskirts of the city.

Every night Yoshi watched his neighbor, Sabu, go to catch eels.

Every day Yoshi watched Sabu broil his eels and wait for customers.

And every evening Yoshi watched a disappointed Sabu eat all the leftover eels.

"The eel broiler should share leftovers with his neighbor," muttered Yoshi.

"The fan maker should buy eels from his neighbor," grumbled Sabu.

But Yoshi loved the sound of coins in his money box too much to buy Sabu's eels.

Instead he sat alone at mealtimes, eating his boiled rice and sniffing Sabu's broiled eels. Yoshi enjoyed with his nose what he would not pay to put in his mouth.

Yoshi sniffed broiled eels for breakfast.

He sniffed broiled eels for lunch.

And he sniffed broiled eels for dinner.

Day in and day out, Yoshi sniffed Sabu's broiled eels for all his meals.

One day Yoshi said to Sabu, "I am glad you broil eels and not cheap stinky fish like samma. Your eels smell delicious!"

Sabu frowned. "When will you buy some?"

"Never!" Yoshi exclaimed, sniffing the air. "Because of your delicious-smelling eels, my money box grows heavier every day."

"How so?" Sabu asked.

"For me, smelling your expensive eels is as good as eating them. Now, the only food I buy is rice." Yoshi grinned. "Because of your eels, I grow richer with every meal."

Sabu stomped his foot.

"Yoshi, you're the reason I am poor. If you had paid me for all the eels you have smelled, my money box would be heavy, too."

And with that, Sabu angrily wrote out a bill.

He presented it to Yoshi, saying, "Neighbor, you owe me for all the broiled eels you have smelled."

Yoshi tapped his chin. "You are right, Sabu. Fair is fair. I will get my money box."

Yoshi carried the heavy metal box over to Sabu and carefully counted the shining mass of gold kobans and silver ichi-bu and ni-bu.

"Here is the amount you say I owe," Yoshi said. But instead of handing over the coins, he placed them back into the box.

Then Yoshi lifted the box
and shook it.

chin chin jara jara...

chin jara jara...

The coins jingled.
Yoshi swayed to the sound.

chin chin jara jara...

He danced in the street.

chin jara jara...

And he danced wildly around and around
Sabu's hibachi.

chin chin jara jara... chin jara jara...

A few people heard the jingling coins and
gathered to watch. They clapped and cheered.
More and more people came until . . .

"STOP!" Sabu yelled.
"Give me my money!"

Yoshi gently touched the eel broiler's bill
with his fan, bowed low, and said,
"But, neighbor, we are even now."

"What?" cried Sabu. "Aren't you going to pay me?"

"I have paid you," Yoshi replied with a smile. "You have charged me for the smell of your eels, and I have paid you with the sound of my money."

Sabu's face turned bright red. "Yoshi, you **will** pay for this!"

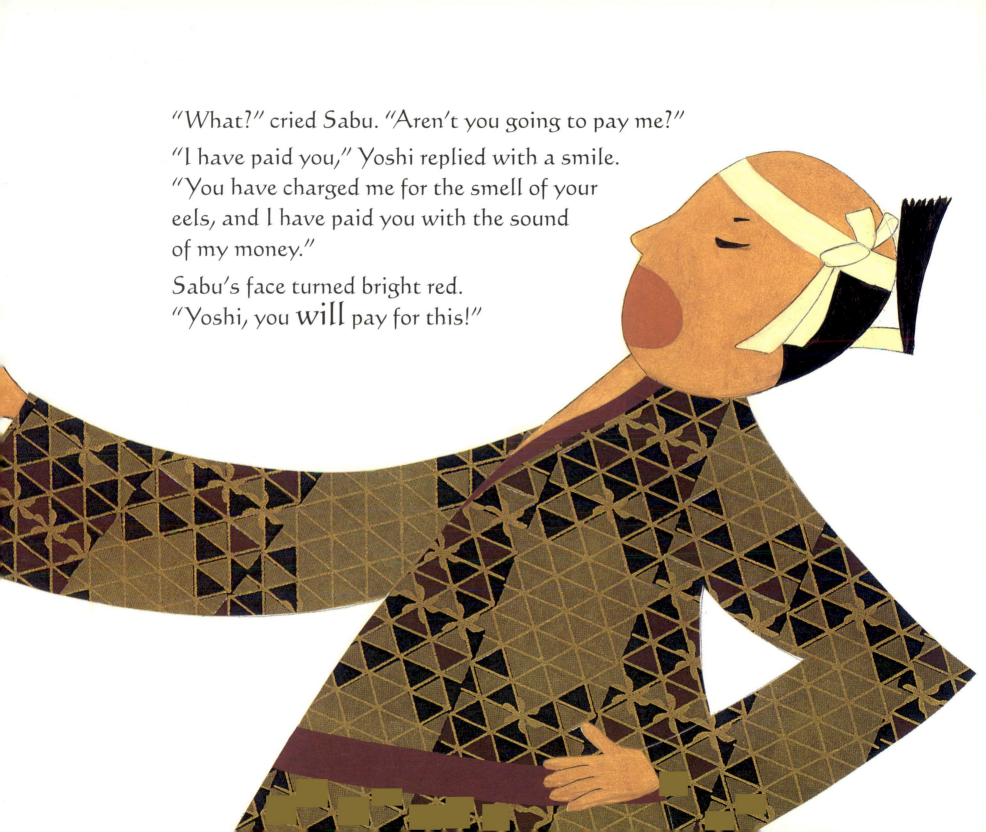

That evening Yoshi waited for Sabu to catch his eels.

But Sabu never left the house.

The next day Yoshi was startled by a horrible smell.

"Kusai!" Yoshi yelled, racing out of his house.

But the smell was even worse outside.

Thick smoke poured from Sabu's hibachi.

"What are you cooking, Sabu?" Yoshi cried.
"The entire city stinks!"

"Samma." Sabu grinned. "Want some?"

Now Yoshi's face turned bright red.
"But samma is the stinkiest fish in all of
Japan! How dare you spoil my appetite?"

This time Sabu laughed.
"Neighbor, you get what you pay for."

Yoshi ran inside his house and boarded up the shoji screens. He fanned and fanned the air, but the smell of stinky fish remained.

Yoshi sniffed stinky samma for breakfast.

He sniffed stinky samma for lunch.

And he sniffed stinky samma for dinner.

Yoshi tried to eat his rice. But the stinky smells made his stomach spin.

Then Yoshi had an idea.

Holding his nose, Yoshi bowed to Sabu.

"Neighbor, I know we've had our differences, but I think we can work them out."

"How so?" Sabu asked.

"Just cook some eels. Then leave it to me and you will see," Yoshi answered.

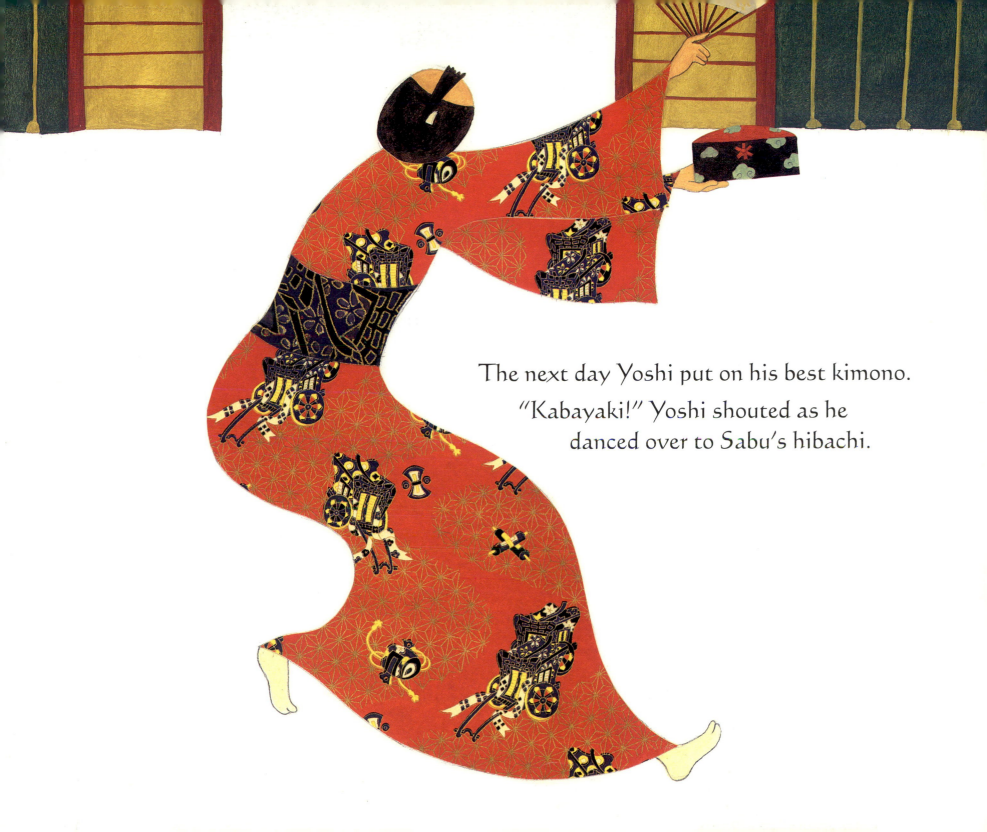

The next day Yoshi put on his best kimono.
"Kabayaki!" Yoshi shouted as he
danced over to Sabu's hibachi.

The smell of Sabu's sizzling eels invigorated Yoshi.
He slithered around Sabu's hibachi.

chin chin jara jara... chin jara jara ...

A crowd gathered and clapped in time to the
jingling coins. Yoshi winked and laughed as he
danced.

chin chin jara jara ...

He spun around, his arms and legs waving wildly—like an electric eel himself.

chin jara jara...

Faster and faster.

chin chin jara jara...

Louder and louder!

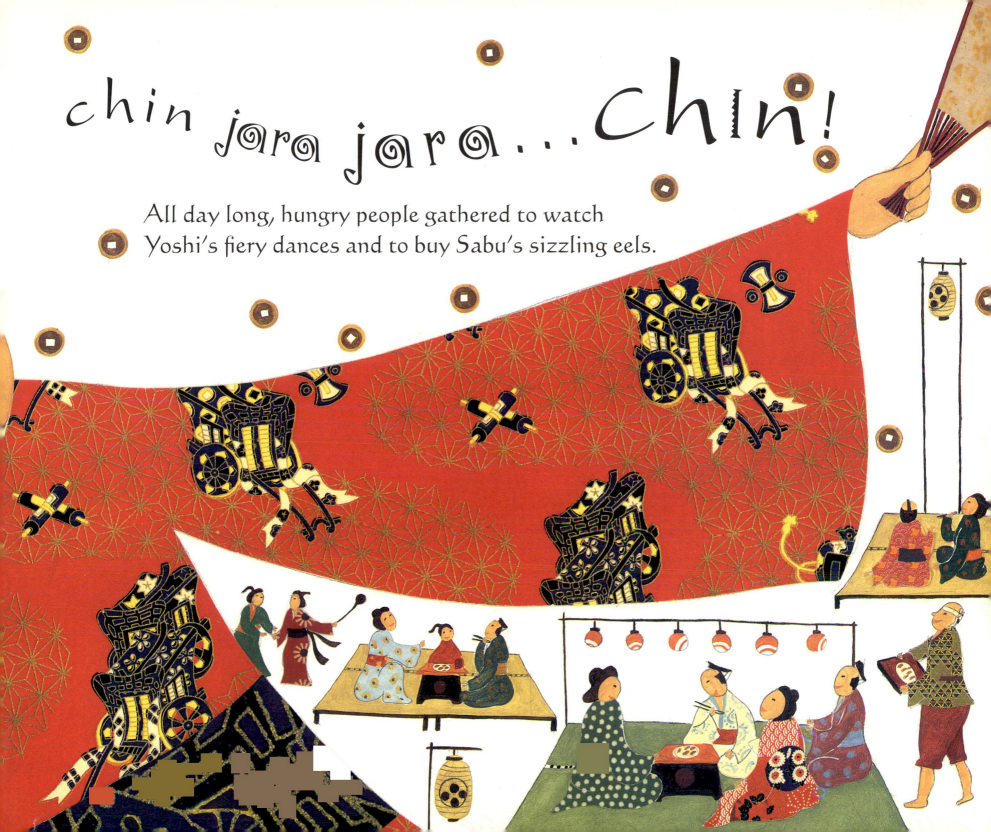

chin jara jara...chin!

All day long, hungry people gathered to watch
Yoshi's fiery dances and to buy Sabu's sizzling eels.

When the day was over, Yoshi prepared his usual meal of boiled rice and green tea. As he sat down to eat, Sabu arrived with a big platter of broiled eels.

"Arigato, neighbor, for bringing me customers."

"Arigato," Yoshi replied, "but I will accept your generous gift only if you join me for dinner."

The two neighbors sat down to eat.

Yoshi picked up an eel and took a big bite. He smiled.

"Mmm! I was wrong!" he exclaimed. "Sniffing broiled eels by myself is nowhere near as good as eating them with a friend."

Every day after that, Yoshi danced for happy
crowds around Sabu's hibachi.

And every evening the two neighbors sat on
Yoshi's porch—laughing and enjoying
Sabu's sizzling-hot eels.

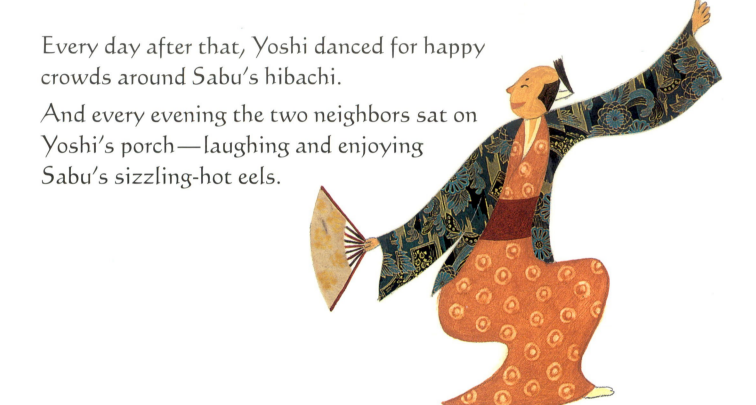